VANESSA KING
WITH VAL PAYNE
& PETER HARPER

ILLUSTRATED BY
CELESTE AIRES

50 WAYS to feel HAPPY

ACTION FOR HAPPINESS

QEB

Quarto is the authority on a wide range of topics.

Quarto educates, entertains and enriches the lives of our readers—enthusiasts and lovers of hands-on living.

www.quartoknows.com

First Published in 2018 by QEB Publishing,
an imprint of The Quarto Group.
6 Orchard Road
Suite 100
Lake Forest, CA 92630
T: +1 949 380 7510
F: +1 949 380 7575
www.QuartoKnows.com

ISBN: 9781682973110

Manufactured in Guangdong, China CC112017

9 8 7 6 5 4 3 2 1

ABOUT THE AUTHORS

Vanessa King

Vanessa is the lead positive psychologist with the charity Action for Happiness and is a member of its Board. Vanessa studied Positive Psychology at the University of Pennsylvania with Dr. Martin Seligman and many other leaders of the field. She is the architect of the *10 Keys to Happier Living*—drawing on science to create a menu of practical actions that have been shown to increase our own, and one another's happiness and resilience. Her book for adults, *10 Keys to Happier Living* is published by Headline.

Peter Harper & Val Payne

Peter is a consultant clinical psychologist and Val is an education consultant and teacher. Both have had and enjoyed many years of experience working with children of all ages. Together they have developed a primary school program based on the 10 Keys to Happier Living which has increased the wellbeing of students, and teachers say it has helped them feel happier too!

CONTENTS

ABOUT THIS BOOK

So you want to explore happiness and find out how to feel happier. What a great idea! Everyone wants to feel happier!

The good news is that scientists have been working on this topic and they have discovered many different activities and ways of thinking that can lead to a happier life for us all.

You might already have some ideas about what helps you to feel happier and this book will help you discover lots more. Whether you're feeling happy right now and want to stay that way or you need some ideas to feel happier, this book is for you. It's packed full of activities to try.

HAPPY

YAY

You'll need to think like an explorer or a scientist. Pick an activity and try it out to see what you discover. Think of it as an experiment—see what you feel and what you notice.

You might want to find a notebook that you keep especially for your experiments and your discoveries.

10 KEYS TO HAPPIER LIVING

Everyone's path to happiness is different. Based on the latest research, experts at Action for Happiness have worked out 10 Keys to Happier Living—the areas where we can take action to help us feel happier and more fulfilled. You'll find that all the activities in this book fit into one of the 10 Keys. There's a chapter for each:

1. GIVING
2. RELATING
3. EXERCISING
4. AWARENESS
5. TRYING OUT
6. DIRECTION
7. RESILIENCE
8. EMOTIONS
9. ACCEPTANCE
10. MEANING

TIPS for STAYING SAFE (and tidy!)

- Always tell your parents or caregiver where you are going and who you are going with.

- Ask your parents or caregiver, or another safe adult to help you with the activities, especially for messy projects or ones you may find difficult.

- Be careful when using scissors or sharp objects.

- Wear old clothes or an apron for "create and make" activities.

SEE PAGE 63 FOR A NOTE TO PARENTS AND CAREGIVERS.

GETTING STARTED

This book is full of activities and ideas to help boost how happy you feel. You can work through them in order or pick out pages at random. Here are two great starting points to begin exploring happiness.

★ THINK FOR A MINUTE

What are all the things that help you feel happy? Think about people, activities, places —anything! There are no wrong answers. You could write or draw them in your notebook. Now think about what really helps you feel happy. What are your top three things?

★ BE A HAPPINESS INVESTIGATOR

We are all different people, so what helps each of us feel happy can be different too. Ask other people to share three things that really help them feel happy.

Ask as many different people as you can. You could ask a friend, your mom, dad, or caregiver, brother or sister; grandparents, aunt, or uncle; or even your teacher. Keep a note of their answers in your notebook.

Now investigate the list you have made. Are there things that lots of people share? How does what they say compare to your list? What's the same and what's different?

HAPPY FACT

Scientists are finding that happiness can do us good. People who feel happy are less likely to catch a cold, they are more likely to help others, more likely do better at school and make friends. When they grow up they might also do better at work and in their relationships too.

SPREAD A LITTLE HAPPINESS!

DOES FEELING HAPPY NEVER MEAN FEELING UNHAPPY?

Can we be happy all the time? Well, that's not realistic. Struggles and difficulties are part of life too. Sometimes things happen that naturally mean we feel sad, angry, upset, or afraid. For example, if a good friend moves away, we don't get something we really wanted, someone is unfriendly to us, or we sense danger.

Living happily isn't about ignoring these feelings but learning how to respond in the most constructive way we can.

There are also times we need to work hard and deal with challenges. This may not feel good at the time, but can lead to feeling happier later. Think about when you've learned something new, maybe a musical instrument, riding a bike, or a new type of sum in math. At first it may have felt really hard, confusing, or frustrating, but once you had finally learned to do it, you felt a real sense of achievement.

The good news is that the activities in this book can also help you cope with difficulties and bounce back more quickly when things go wrong. That's all part of happier living!

Now let's get started on unlocking the secrets to feeling happier—see what you can discover!

1 GIVING

DO KIND THINGS FOR OTHERS

Isn't it funny that the very first key to happier living is about other people's happiness rather than our own?

Well, scientists have found that when we do kind things for others, not only does it help them to feel happier, we feel happier too. In fact, science shows that helping others can have the same effect on our brain as receiving a gift ourselves or eating our favorite food! Helping others can also take our mind off our own worries.

HAPPY FACT

In an experiment people were asked to do five new acts of kindness in one day (things they didn't already do). They felt happier for up to six weeks afterward!

QUICK START: MAKE TODAY A KINDNESS DAY

What kind things can you do today (or even right now) to help or be nice to someone else? Here are some ideas to get you started...

★ Open a door or carry a bag for someone.

★ Clear the table without being asked.

★ Offer to help your teacher or someone at home.

★ Give a friend a hug or a high five.

★ Draw a picture and give it to a friend.

★ Say something nice to someone.

★ Smile at someone.

★ Say thank you to people who do things for you but aren't always thanked—perhaps your teacher, the bus driver, or your mom or dad!

HOW KIND!

WHAT OTHER THINGS COULD YOU TRY TODAY? CAN YOU TRY TO DO AT LEAST FIVE KIND THINGS?

1. THE POWER OF KINDNESS

Think about a time when someone has been kind to you:

★ What was the situation? What did they do? What did you feel?

★ Next time you see the person, remind them what they did and thank them.

WHEN YOU..........................

I FELT..............................

THANK YOU!

2. THE "MANY WAYS OF BEING KIND" CHALLENGE

Make a list of all the ways you could be kind or help other people. Some things will be quick and easy; others will be harder or take longer.

How many ideas can you think of right now? Keep thinking and add to your list—can you get to 100 different ways of being kind, giving, or helping people?

Now take the challenge to the next level. Your goal is to do everything on your list! It may take a few weeks or even months and you might need help with some things, but give it your best shot—how many can you do? Make sure you check your list with a safe adult before you start.

Don't forget to check off everything you've tried!

Some ways of being kind

★ Be friendly to a new kid at school.

★ Organize something to raise money for charity.

★ Offer to walk a neighbor's dog.

★ Offer to clean your room so your parents don't have to moan at you!

★ Write a letter to say hello and brighten the day of a grandparent, aunt, or uncle that you don't often see.

★ Bake cakes (ask for help from an adult) and give them to elderly neighbors who live alone.

★ Stop yourself from being mean to someone and say something kind instead.

★ Find out where your nearest food bank is and ask your family, neighbors, and friends to help you collect food to take there.

ASK AN ADULT

3. SET UP A KINDNESS BOX AT HOME

Ask an adult for a box to keep at home. This is a place where you and your family can put messages, photos, stories, drawings, or thank-you notes about the kind things people have done for them or they've seen done for others.

★ You may want to label or decorate the box.

★ Find time to share the contents of the box with everyone.

ASK AN ADULT

4. BECOME A KINDNESS DETECTIVE

Over the next week, look out for acts of kindness or helping happening around you. Make a note of each act of kindness or giving that you see during a whole week. For example:

WHO	WHAT	HOW	WHERE	WHEN	WHY
Jenny	Helped Dad prepare dinner	She buttered the bread and set the table	At home	Saturday	So Dad didn't have too much to do

5. GIVING AWARDS

YOU WILL NEED:

- Letter-size sheet of cardstock or paper
- Colored markers or pencils

CREATE AND MAKE

Once you've been a kindness detective and spotted lots of ways people around you are kind or help others, you can give them something—a Giving Award!

For each person on your kindness list, create a certificate. You may want to decorate it or draw a picture of the person they helped or what they did.

GIVING AWARD

This certificate is awarded to: ....

For their acts of kindness: ....

....

THANK YOU FOR YOUR KINDNESS!

TIME FOR THE AWARD CEREMONY

- ★ Invite everyone at home to attend an award ceremony.
- ★ Explain that it's to celebrate acts of kindness.
- ★ Choose a time when everyone can be there, perhaps after an evening meal.
- ★ Decide a place where the ceremony will be held, such as the living room.
- ★ Present a certificate to everyone at home during the ceremony.

6. GIVE COMPLIMENT CARDS

YOU WILL NEED:

- Letter-size sheet of cardstock or paper
- Colored pencils and pens
- Scissors

A compliment is an expression of admiration or praise toward someone. Think about what you feel when someone says something nice to you. It feels good, doesn't it?

However, we often notice or appreciate positive qualities about another person but don't tell them. Making and giving compliment cards is a good way of helping another person to feel good!

HOW TO DO IT:

1 Divide your sheet of cardstock or paper into 12 equal-sized boxes (to make 12 compliment cards).

2 Decide on what compliments you want to give out, such as "I love your smile!"; "You're amazing!"; "You're a great sister!"

I LOVE YOUR SMILE!

YOU'RE AMAZING!

YOU'RE A GREAT SISTER!

3 Write your compliments onto your cards (you can use the same words on several cards).

4 Decorate your cards so that they are colorful.

5 Cut the cards out.

6 Give them to the people you want to compliment.

7 If you feel brave, say the compliment to them as you give them the card.

8 You may want to keep some cards in your pocket, ready to give when you spot someone you want to give a compliment to!

7. MAKE A FRIENDSHIP SCRAPBOOK

YOU WILL NEED:

- A scrapbook, empty photo album, or notebook. Or you could make your own by gathering several sheets of cardstock or paper, making holes with a hole punch, and tying the pages together with string or a ribbon.
- Scissors
- Glue or tape
- Paint or colored pens
- Stickers, glitter, etc. to decorate

Create and fill a friendship scrapbook to give to one of your friends or someone else you care about, to remind them of the good times you've shared together.

A HANDMADE GIFT THAT SHOWS YOU'VE REALLY THOUGHT ABOUT SOMEONE IS VERY SPECIAL AND DOESN'T NEED TO COST MUCH MONEY.

CREATE AND MAKE

HOW TO DO IT:

1 Find a selection of photos of you and your friend, things that you both like, places you've been or want to go, or things that mean something to you both. You could also gather pictures from magazines, tickets, and any souvenirs.

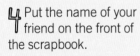

2 Glue or tape the photos and pictures onto the pages of your scrapbook.

3 You could paint or draw pictures as well.

4 Put the name of your friend on the front of the scrapbook.

5 To make it extra special, decorate the cover with stickers, glitter, or whatever you like.

DAISY

2 RELATING

CONNECT WITH PEOPLE

Feeling connected to other people is very important for our happiness—even if we are shy!

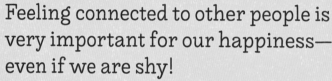

This doesn't mean we need to get along with everyone, but having at least a few people that we trust and can share things with matters for our happiness. This may include members of our family and our close friends.

We can learn skills to help us build good connections, to help us feel cared for, and be able to care for others too.

HAPPY FACT

Scientists have found that we are 30 times more likely to laugh when we are with another person than when we are on our own!

QUICK START: STOP-LOOK-LISTEN

Learning to listen well to others is a great foundation to build good relationships. It's a quick skill that you can practice right away...

When someone speaks to you:

★ STOP what you are doing and give your full attention to the speaker.

★ LOOK at them and smile in a friendly way.

★ LISTEN carefully to what they say and how they say it.

★ WAIT until they have finished before you reply. When they have spoken, ask one or two questions to show you are interested.

BEING A CAREFUL LISTENER SHOWS THAT YOU CARE.

8. MY VIPs (VERY IMPORTANT PEOPLE)

Celebrate the important people in your life by making them a special VIP badge or sticker.

YOU WILL NEED:

- Letter-size sheet of cardstock or paper
- Blank sticky labels or, if you're making badges, safety pins and tape
- Pens

HOW TO DO IT:

1 Make a list of three or four people who are very important to you (your VIPs).

2 Write down some words that describe the qualities that make them special to you.

ASK AN ADULT

YOU'RE A VIP
SMART

YOU'RE A VIP
CARING

YOU'RE A VIP
LOYAL

YOU'RE A VIP
FUNNY

Smart
Caring
Loyal
Funny

3 Make and decorate a sticker or badge for each of your VIPs. Write the qualities that you most appreciate.

CREATE AND MAKE

YOU ALWAYS LOOK AFTER ME

YOU'RE A GREAT FRIEND

4 Give these to each of your VIPs, telling them the qualities you most value.

9. BECOME A REPORTER: INTERVIEW A FRIEND

Friendships are important for happiness. Doing fun things together, sharing your worries, celebrating your good news, and learning about each other are all part of building friendships.

How much do you know about your friends?

Imagine you are a reporter for your local newspaper and ask a friend if you can interview them to find out more about them.

Here are some questions that you might ask...

★ What is your favorite book?

★ What is your favorite food?

★ What is your favorite game?

★ What are you enjoying most about school at the moment?

★ What do you like most about the town/city/village you live in?

★ What are your top interests and hobbies?

★ What has been your happiest moment?

★ What are you most proud of?

★ What advice would you give to people so that they could feel happier?

★ Who would you include on your own VIP (Very Important People) list? What makes them special to you?

PAUSE FOR THOUGHT:
WHAT NEW THINGS DID YOU LEARN ABOUT YOUR FRIEND?

book

food

game

10. CURIOUS CONVERSATIONS

YOU WILL NEED:

- Letter-size sheet of cardstock or paper
- Pencil and ruler
- Scissors
- Colored pens

A conversation is an exchange of ideas—it involves listening to what others have to say as well as sharing your own thoughts. Create these fun cards to boost your conversation skills. Gather some friends, shuffle the cards, read out the questions, and take turns to answer. Be imaginative and have fun. Remember, there are no wrong answers. Be sure to listen well to each other's ideas.

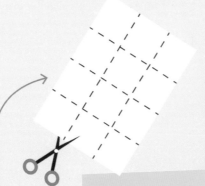

HOW TO MAKE YOUR CARDS:

1 Divide the A4 cardstock into 12 equal-sized boxes.

2 Cut them out so you have 12 small cards.

3 On each card, write a question or topic to discuss with your friends. You can use the list on this page, or make up your own. The aim is that each card will start a conversation, but they can be as silly as you like!

BE A GOOD LISTENER

Listening is a really important happiness skill as it shows you care about and are interested in what other people are saying, not just in what you have to say! Look back to page 14 for some great ideas to try.

CURIOUS QUESTION IDEAS:

1. If you could be any animal, what would you be?
2. Would you rather live in the future, or the past?
3. If you could give away your allowance to do good in the world, who or what would you help?
4. Would you rather go to space or to the bottom of the ocean?
5. Would you rather be an amazing painter or a brilliant mathematician?
6. If you could go anywhere in the world, where would you go?
7. Would you rather have hands for feet or feet for hands?
8. Would you rather live on a boat or in a treehouse?
9. If you could have any super power, what would it be?
10. Would you rather only be able to eat your favorite food for the rest of your life or never eat your favorite food again?
11. If you could have any pet, what would you choose?
12. Would you rather have a flying carpet or a car that can drive underwater?

11. MAKE A SURPRISE UN-BIRTHDAY CARD FOR SOMEONE SPECIAL

YOU WILL NEED:

- Letter-size sheet of cardstock
- Letter-size sheet of colored paper
- Sheet of white paper
- Paints, pencil, crayons
- Pen
- Glue
- Scissors

CREATE AND MAKE

We all like to get cards on our birthday, but why should it be only then? Let someone special know you are thinking of them by surprising them with an un-birthday card you've made! You might have ideas for the card you want to make or you could try making a tree card like the one below...

HOW TO MAKE A TREE CARD:

1 Decide who you are making the card for.

2 Fold your cardstock in half.

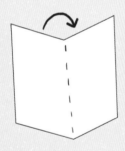

3 Cut a piece of colored paper that will fit onto the front of the card, leaving a small white frame around the edge.

5 Cut another piece of white paper to fit onto the colored piece, leaving a small colored frame around the edge. Glue the white paper into place.

6 Draw a tree trunk and branches on the white paper. This could be a simple shape, such as a triangle on a square, or something more fancy.

7 Create leaves for the tree. You could do this by making "finger print leaves," or cutting out leaf shapes and sticking them on.

8 Complete your picture by including birds, the sky, stars, the sun or moon, or flowers.

9 Add words to your card to personalize it, e.g. "HAPPY UN-BIRTHDAY!; Thank you for...; You're great!," or simply write the name of the person you are giving the card to.

10 Write a message inside the card.

11 Give your card to your chosen person.

4 Glue the colored paper into place.

3 EXERCISING

TAKE CARE OF YOUR BODY

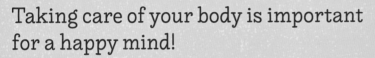

Taking care of your body is important for a happy mind!

Taking care of your body helps you to stay physically healthy and it's also important for your happiness. You can take care of your body in three main ways:

★ Moving more and sitting less.
★ Eating healthily (lots of fruit and vegetables and not much sugar).
★ Getting enough sleep.

HAPPY FACT

Scientists have found that exercising regularly can improve brain power and help us learn. It can boost our confidence too!

QUICK START: GET MOVING

Exercising regularly and sitting less is important for happiness and feeling healthy.

So start now! Try hula hooping, jumping jacks, doing handstands, dancing energetically, or running on the spot for one minute as fast as you can.

SET AN ALARM TO REMIND YOU TO GET UP AND MOVE EVERY 30 MINUTES WHEN YOU ARE AT HOME.

What do you feel afterward?

★ OUT OF BREATH?
★ MORE AWAKE?
★ MORE ENERGIZED?
★ HAPPIER?
★ ALL OF THE ABOVE?

THINK ABOUT IT: WHICH TYPES OF EXERCISE DO YOU ENJOY MOST? COULD YOU DO A LITTLE EVERY DAY?

12. CIRCUIT 100 CHALLENGE

Choose a place where you have some space to move around. This could be a room at home, a garden, a park, or a playground.

Your aim is to do each of the four activities below and complete a circuit of one hundred movements. Make sure you count along!

1. Do 25 jumping jacks.
2. Run on the spot for 25 steps.
3. Do 25 hops on one leg.
4. Reach down and touch your toes 25 times.

Time how long it takes you to do a set of all four activities. Try to do your circuit every day and see how your time improves as your fitness improves.

IF YOU GO TO A PARK OR PLAYGROUND, MAKE SURE YOU ASK YOUR PARENT OR CAREGIVER FIRST.

ASK AN ADULT

13. TASTE TEST TRIAL

Gather your siblings or friends, and have a taste testing trial! Ask an adult to prepare at least five fruits and five vegetables you haven't tried before. Give a piece of each food to every player.

Try each one in turn...

★ Shut your eyes, or wear a blindfold, so that you can concentrate on the taste.

★ Take a bite and chew well.

★ Award 10 points for each food tried.

★ How many points did everyone score?

★ Which was your favorite?

★ Which will you eat again?

14. EAT A RAINBOW: MAKE YOUR OWN FRUIT STICKS

YOU WILL NEED:

- A selection of colorful fruits
- Kitchen roll
- Wooden kebab skewers or sticks
- Cutting board
- Kitchen knife

To have a healthy diet with lots of good nutrients and vitamins, it's important to try to eat a variety of different colored fruits and vegetables every day. Here's a colorful recipe to try...

ASK AN ADULT

HOW TO DO IT:

1 Gather a variety of colorful fruits. For example, strawberries, an orange, a pineapple, a mango, kiwi fruit, grapes, blueberries, blackberries, raspberries…

Can you find one fruit for each color of the rainbow?

2 Wash the fruit and pat dry with a paper towel.

3 Ask an adult to help you chop up the larger fruits into small chunks, using a kitchen knife and a cutting board.

4 Make a pile of each type of fruit and start adding them to your kebab sticks.

5 Fill each stick with a mixture of fruits and if you like, use the colors to try out some different patterns.

6 Share your fruit sticks with friends or family!

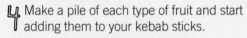

For another tasty treat, why not try making rainbow vegetable kebabs too? Ask an adult to cook these on a BBQ or grill for you.

15. HAPPY SLEEP HABITS

Make sleep your superpower! Scientists say children need at least nine hours of sleep every night to feel happy and stay healthy.

Getting a good night's sleep is important for happiness. If we have too little sleep, it can make us grumpy, easily upset, and less able to concentrate and learn. It can also mean we want to eat sugary foods that aren't good for us and make us less likely to want to exercise.

Can you find a bedtime routine to make sure you get a good night's sleep every night?

TIPS FOR GOOD SLEEP

★ Try and stick to a regular bedtime, to help you get to sleep faster and sleep better.

★ Have a milky drink an hour before bedtime.

★ Make your bedtime space cozy, quiet, and dark—light and noise can keep your brain wide awake, making it harder to fall asleep.

★ Switch off your tech! Devices like phones, tablets, and laptops give out a blue light that makes your brain think it's daytime, keeping you awake. Apps, games, and messaging keep your mind whirring rather than letting it rest. So switch these all off an hour before you want to sleep and read a book instead.

16. HAPPY GAMES EVENT

YOU WILL NEED:

- Equipment for the games (ball, soccer ball, jump rope, potato, spoon, obstacles, etc.)
- Sheets of paper
- Pens

Gather your friends, head outside, and throw a Happy Games event! You'll have lots of fun, as well as discovering the benefits of outdoor exercise.

ASK AN ADULT

IDEAS FOR ACTIVITIES:

★ THROW, CLAP & CATCH—How many times can you throw a ball up in the air and catch it again, clapping three times after each throw?

★ UP IN THE AIR—How many times can you keep a soccer ball in the air, bouncing it only on your knees?

★ SKIP AND SING—Who can skip on the spot for the longest time while singing a song?

★ HOPPING RELAY—In teams, have a hopping relay race while throwing and catching a ball at the same time.

★ POTATO AND SPOON RACE—Race while balancing a potato on a spoon and stepping over small obstacles.

GIVE A "HAPPY SCORE"!

★ After each activity, ask everyone to give themselves a happiness score out of 10 to show how much they enjoyed it. The higher the number, the happier the activity!

★ You could even make everyone a set of score cards and ask each person to hold up their happiness score after each activity.

★ Spread the word! Tell others about the benefits of holding a Happy Games event.

MAXIMIZE YOUR MOVING!

Health experts say kids need to do at least 60 minutes of moderate to high intensity physical activity every day.

MODERATE INTENSITY activities include:
- ★ walking to school
- ★ riding a scooter
- ★ skateboarding
- ★ walking the dog
- ★ cycling on flat ground

HIGH INTENSITY activities include:
- ★ swimming
- ★ running
- ★ playing chase or football
- ★ dancing energetically
- ★ cycling fast or uphill

It's good to do activities that make your muscles and bones stronger as well, such as: climbing, tennis, skipping, hopscotch, and gymnastics. Try to do some of these activities at least three times per week.

4 AWARENESS

LIVE LIFE MINDFULLY

The past is history, tomorrow is a mystery, today is a gift—that's why it's called the present!

The skill of focusing your attention on the present—what you are doing, what's around you, or who you are talking to—is an important skill for happiness. Everyone's mind naturally wanders but if you can train yourself to focus your attention more mindfully on the present, it can help you to feel calm. It sounds easy but it takes practice! The good news is, you can practice being more mindful in lots of ways.

HAPPY FACT

Scientists have found that our mind wanders at least 50% of the time and that we feel less happy when our mind is wandering than when it's focused on the present.

QUICK START: FOCUS ON THE PRESENT

Here's a quick way to focus on the present...

Right now, ask yourself:
★ What you can see around you?
★ What you can hear?
★ What you can smell?
★ Are you are hot or cold, or just right?
★ What sensations can you feel in your hands and feet, and the rest of your body?

PAUSE FOR THOUGHT: WHAT THINGS DID YOU NOTICE THAT YOU DON'T USUALLY NOTICE?

17. THE MINDFUL MINUTE EXPERIMENT

The mindful minute can be great to try if you are anxious, angry, or upset and can help you feel calm. Spend 60 seconds focusing only on your breath.

GET SET UP:

★ Find a quiet place.

★ Sit on a chair with both feet on the ground and your back straight but not stiff.

★ Place your hands on your knees.

★ Set a timer for one minute.

★ If you can, close your eyes.

TRYING A MINDFUL MINUTE

★ Breathe at a steady pace. You may want to close your eyes.

★ Focus on the tip of your nose.

★ Notice how your breath feels on the tip of your nose as you breathe in...and as you breathe out.

★ If your mind wanders, don't worry—when it does just bring your attention back to your breath.

When the minute is up, open your eyes and notice what you feel. Think about these questions:

★ Was it hard to stay focused on your breath?

★ Did your mind wander?

★ Did you notice where your mind went?

★ When your mind wandered, were you able to bring it back to focus on your breath again?

TIP
Remember, this is like gym for the mind: the more you practice, the better you'll get at keeping your attention on the present—your breath. You could try it out once a day.

18. TAKE A MINDFUL WALK

Mindful walking can be a good way of practicing "noticing and being present." Next time you go out for a walk, such as a walk to school, practice these things...

AS YOU STEP OUTSIDE:

★ NOTICE what the air feels like on your skin. Is it warm or cold?

★ LOOK up at the sky. What can you see? Is it sunny or is it rainy?

ASK AN ADULT

DURING YOUR WALK:

★ NOTICE what the ground feels like under your feet.

★ NOTICE the shapes and colors around you.

★ NOTICE any smells or scents.

★ LISTEN for any sounds. What noises can you hear?

YOU CAN TRY DIFFERENT MINDFUL WALKING ACTIVITIES. FOR EXAMPLE, LOOKING OUT FOR AS MANY DIFFERENT THINGS YOU CAN NOTICE OF A PARTICULAR COLOR OR SHAPE.

AFTER YOUR WALK:

★ DRAW a picture of something beautiful you noticed.

19. MINDFUL EATING

M indful eating is another way you can practice mindfully focusing your attention...

TAKE YOUR TIME AND GIVE YOURSELF 5 TO 10 MINUTES FOR THIS ACTIVITY...

GETTING STARTED:

★ Ask for a small piece of fruit to eat, such as a single grape, slice of apple, or a strawberry.

★ Sit at a table.

★ Turn the TV and your phone off.

ASK AN ADULT

1 LOOK at the fruit really carefully. Notice its shape, size, and all the different colors you can see in it.

2 PICK UP the fruit:
- What can you feel?
- Is it hard or soft, smooth or bumpy?
- What else can you feel?
- What can you smell?

3 Now take a small BITE:
- Listen to the sound as you bite it.
- Before you start to chew, notice what you taste and what you can feel.
- Slowly start chewing—what do you notice?
- How do the taste and the texture change as you chew?
- How slowly can you chew?
- How long before you swallow it?

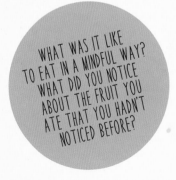

WHAT WAS IT LIKE TO EAT IN A MINDFUL WAY? WHAT DID YOU NOTICE ABOUT THE FRUIT YOU ATE THAT YOU HADN'T NOTICED BEFORE?

20. MINDFUL OR MIND FULL?

People often think that being able to do lots of things at the same time will get more done. However, research shows that exactly the opposite is true. By being mindful and focusing on one thing at a time, you can get much more done and it can help you to feel calmer.

Think about it:
Do you often try to do lots of things at the same time and does it feel like your brain is overflowing with thoughts and feelings?

Draw a picture to show what it's like to have your mind full in this way. Then **draw a second picture** to show what your mind is like when you feel calm and focused.

CREATE AND MAKE

Look at your pictures:
★ Which version shows your mind right now?
★ When is your MIND FULL?
★ When are you MINDFUL?
★ What could you do differently so that you feel MINDFUL more often?

TOP MINDFUL TIPS

If you ever feel like you need to clear your head, try...
★ The mindful minute (see page 25).
★ Counting back from 100 in twos (100, 98, 96...).
★ Picking a topic and thinking of an example for every letter of the alphabet (e.g. animals—ant, bat, cat, dog...).

(PSSST! These activities can help you sleep too!)

21. START YOUR DAY THE MINDFUL WAY

Do you often wake up and rush to get on with your day? Do you switch on your devices as soon as you can? Experiment with starting your day in a more mindful way and notice what you feel as a result. Pick a day and give these activities a try...

WHAT DIFFERENCES DID HAVING A MINDFUL START TO THE DAY MAKE?

WAKING UP

★ Lie in bed, stretch, and wiggle your fingers and toes. Notice how that feels.

★ Sit up and notice three things that you like in the room.

★ Get up, have a big stretch, and shake out your arms and legs. Notice how that feels.

★ Take a big breath in...and breathe out very slowly...

GETTING READY

★ Pay attention to the temperature, sound, and feel of the water as you shower or wash.

★ Notice the smell of the soap you use.

★ How does the towel feel as you dry yourself?

★ As you get dressed, notice how each item of your clothing feels and sounds as you put it on.

★ Breathe in deeply...and then out.

MINDFUL BREAKFAST

★ Turn off your gadgets.

★ Eat slowly and mindfully.

★ Notice the feel, smell, and taste of each mouthful. Do they change as you chew slowly?

★ Carefully wash and put your dish or plate away. Notice any sounds, smells, or textures as you do this.

ON THE WAY TO SCHOOL

★ Listen to and look at your surroundings.
   Notice:
   • the scenery;
   • the people;
   • the sounds;
   • the smells;
   • the colors you can see.

★ Before your first lesson starts, take a moment to focus on your breath to help you get ready to listen and learn.

WHAT COULD YOU DO TO START EVERY DAY MINDFULLY?

5 TRYING OUT

KEEP LEARNING NEW THINGS

You might think learning is just something you do at school, or that it is something boring that adults make you do, but learning new things can actually bring you happiness! You can learn all the time through playing games, having hobbies, exploring, reading, and being curious and creative.

Learning can be challenging and it may not feel good at the time. But if you keep on trying, you will feel proud when you've learned something new. That's part of happiness too.

REMEMBER TO KEEP TRYING! THE MORE YOU PRACTICE THE BETTER YOU'LL GET!

THE POWER OF "YET!"

Instead of saying "I can't do this" or "I'm no good at this," adding the word "yet" can mean we keep trying and get less frustrated with ourselves. So remember to add yet!… "I can't do this…**yet**" or "I'm no good at this…**yet**!"

QUICK START: LEARNING AND FEELING

Ask yourself:

★ **What do you love to learn?** For example: your favorite subject at school, a hobby you haven't tried before, or new dance steps. How many things can you think of?

★ What is **one** thing that you found hard to learn but eventually succeeded in doing?

★ What is **one** thing you've tried for the first time recently?

★ What do you feel when you've succeeded at something new?

★ Do you feel the same for learning different activities?

22. TRY OUT SOMETHING NEW

Trying something new can be a bit scary at first, but it can also be lots of fun and a source of ideas. Here are some new things to try...

MAKE A LIST OF NEW THINGS TO TRY. HOW MANY CAN YOU THINK OF? BE SURE TO ASK AN ADULT BEFORE YOU TRY THEM!

★ Create a new outfit from recycling old clothes and accessories.

★ Start a new hobby.

★ Learn a new game.

★ Listen to and learn a song by a musician you've never heard before.

★ Take a different route to school (ask an adult first).

TIP

If you're having trouble learning something, try making it into a game.

23. CREATE A CURIOSITY COLLAGE

Get curious and create a collage for your wall. Next time you're out for a walk or on your way to school, look up high and look down low.

Collect small items such as leaves, take some photographs, or draw pictures of all the new things you have seen or found. Attach them to a big sheet of paper, label them, and decorate your curious collection.

You could get even more curious and find out a fact about each item you've collected and add these to your collage!

24. LEARN A NEW SKILL: ORIGAMI

Origami is the ancient Japanese art of paper folding. Start by learning to make this simple dog's head. Then, as you get more skilled you can make lots more amazing things!

YOU WILL NEED:

- Square piece of paper (if you only have rectangular paper, you can trim off one edge to make it a square)
- Colored markers, scraps of paper, or decorations
- Glue

CREATE AND MAKE

BE CURIOUS! FIND OUT HOW TO MAKE OTHER ORIGAMI ANIMALS BY RESEARCHING ON THE INTERNET OR IN A BOOK.

HOW TO MAKE:

1 Fold your square of paper in half so that it forms a triangle. Crease it carefully along the fold.

2 Fold the triangle in half again. Crease. Open back out again.

3 Turn the triangle so that the long side is at the top facing away from you. Fold one of the corners down to form an ear.

4 Fold the other corner down to form another ear. Make sure the ears are the same size.

5 Now fold the bottom point up, to give your dog a nose.

6 Use colored markers to add eyes and whiskers, and glue on scraps of colored paper or decorations to bring your dog to life.

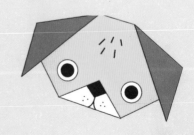

25. SPARK UP YOUR CREATIVITY!

Imagine you're an alien who has just arrived on Earth from another planet. You see a sock for the first time but don't know that it goes on a foot (you may not even have seen a foot!).

How many creative ways can you think of to use the sock?

HAPPY FACT
When we are in a good mood we often generate more ideas!

...a hat

...a bag

...a puppet

...a flag

THERE'S NO SUCH THING AS A BAD IDEA IN THIS CHALLENGE. LET YOUR IMAGINATION RUN FREE!

BREAK THE RULES!

Think of a game you like to play. How can you be creative and change the rules to make a new game? Give it a try!

26. SKILLS SWAP SHOP

Everyone has something they can teach to others and you can learn a lot from the people around you. Set up an event where people can swap their skills so that everyone can try something new.

SETTING UP A SKILLS SWAP SHOP

1 Invite friends and family to your "Skills Swap Shop."

2 Ask them to come prepared to share a skill or something they have learned.

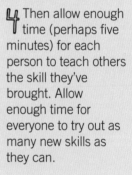

ASK AN ADULT

CIAO

SVEIKI

HI

HOLA

BONJOUR

3 When you are together, give each person in turn a minute or two to show the skill they've brought.

4 Then allow enough time (perhaps five minutes) for each person to teach others the skill they've brought. Allow enough time for everyone to try out as many new skills as they can.

SHARE HAPPINESS BY SHARING AND LEARNING SKILLS!

6 DIRECTION

MY DREAMS →

HAVE GOALS TO LOOK FORWARD TO

Having goals to work toward and look forward to is an important part of happiness. Goals are the stepping stones that will take you from where you are now to where you want to be, and will help you turn your dreams into a reality.

Your goals can be as small as planning what to do tomorrow, or as big as setting out to learn a new skill or visit a new place, or even planning the career you want when you're older.

It's not just reaching our goals that brings happiness. Setting and planning how we can reach them can help us feel happy, too!

QUICK START: TAKE A FIRST STEP

Often the hardest part of reaching a goal is getting started. Even if your dream is big, you can start to achieve it by taking one small step.

★ Pick **one small thing** you could do today that is a step toward one of your dreams...and do it! For example, if you want to visit Paris, find out about different ways to get there or write a list of the things you would like to see and do.

DO YOU HAVE A DREAM? IF YOU COULD BE OR DO ANYTHING YOU WANT, WHAT WOULD YOU CHOOSE?

"A JOURNEY OF A THOUSAND MILES STARTS WITH ONE STEP."
ANCIENT PROVERB

27. DREAM RECIPE

Y ou can start turning a dream into reality right now by thinking about the small steps you will need to take to make it happen, and the ingredients you may need along the way. Think of it like a recipe for baking a cake!

Write a recipe for one of your dreams. Ask a friend to do the same and find out about each other's dreams.

MY DREAM IS TO PLAY THE GUITAR

YOU WILL NEED:

- A guitar
- A teacher (in person or online)
- Some music
- A place and time to practice

If you create a clear picture in your mind about where, when, and how you'll take your next step toward your goal, you are more likely to actually take that step and get closer to achieving your goal!

METHOD (What are the steps you could follow to put these ingredients together?):

1 Research where to find, borrow, or buy a guitar.

2 Look up local teachers and ask your parents or caregiver about contacting them for lessons. You could also look up lessons on YouTube and teach yourself, or ask a friend who can play to help you learn.

3 Identify three songs you'd like to be able to play.

4 Plan when and where you will practice. Agree this with your parents or caregiver.

28. ME IN THE FUTURE

It can be helpful to have a vision of what you would like your future to be. It may not always become a reality, but if you have a picture of where you want to be, you can set goals for how to get there. So it's more likely you can make your dream future come true!

Imagine yourself in 10 years' time. How old will you be? What are you doing? Who are you with? Where do you live? Draw a picture of what you imagine.

29. ROLL A GOAL!

Think about one of your goals and the steps you might need to reach it. Make your own die using a letter-size sheet of cardstock, glue, scissors, and the template here as a guide. Each square should be about 2.5 x 2.5 inches (6x6 cm). Write an activity on each side of the die that will help you achieve your goal. Roll your die every day and do the step or activity that it lands on. For instance, if you want to be a soccer player...

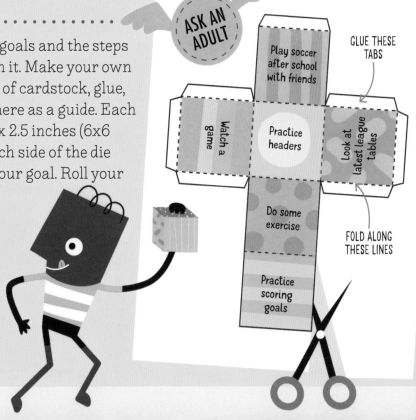

ASK AN ADULT

Play soccer after school with friends

Watch a game

Practice headers

Look at latest league tables

Do some exercise

Practice scoring goals

GLUE THESE TABS

FOLD ALONG THESE LINES

30. MAKE A MEDAL

Design and make a medal to award to yourself for something that you've achieved. It can be hard work trying to reach goals, so it's important to have mini celebrations as you achieve steps along the way. This can help you to keep motivated and see the progress you have made.

CREATE AND MAKE

YOU WILL NEED:

- Cardstock
- Scissors
- Colored pens
- Glitter
- Hole punch
- Ribbon

HOW TO MAKE A MEDAL

I PLAYED MY FIRST SONG

I PLAYED MY FIRST SONG

I PLAYED MY FIRST SONG

1 Cut out a circle shape from your piece of cardstock.

2 Write your achievement in the middle. Remember to leave room for the decorations!

3 Decorate your medal however you wish!

4 Punch a hole through the top.

5 Thread a length of ribbon through the hole, long enough to tie around your neck.

6 Wear your medal with pride!

I PLAYED MY FIRST SONG

THINK ABOUT IT

Celebrating is not just for winning. We can celebrate other things too, such as finding a way to overcome an obstacle, having a great idea, having persistence to keep going when things were hard, or even helping someone else achieve their goal.

YOU COULD EVEN MAKE MEDALS FOR YOUR FRIENDS AND FAMILY TO CELEBRATE THEIR GOALS!

31. CREATE A MOUNTAIN OBSTACLE COURSE

As with mountain climbing, your progress toward your goals may not always go smoothly. Obstacles may get in your way, and overcoming them is all part of the adventure.

On a big piece of paper, create a mountain obstacle course poster that shows one of your goals at the top, the obstacles that could get in your way, and ways to deal with them.

Draw yourself on a separate piece of paper or cut out a photograph of yourself. You can move this picture up your mountain as you achieve your goals. Remember to celebrate after getting past each obstacle and when you reach the top!

GOAL!

TIP
If you're prepared for obstacles, they are easier to handle!

OBSTACLE 3
What is it?
How will I beat it?

OBSTACLE 2
What is it?
How will I beat it?

TAKE ACTION
Begin your journey up the mountain path to reach your goal.

THIS WAY

OBSTACLE 1
What is it?
How will I beat it?

START!

DO THE RESEARCH
What skills, materials and equipment, etc. will you need to reach your goal?

PLAN YOUR SUPPORT
Who or what might help you to reach your goal?

7 RESILIENCE

...wheeee

FIND WAYS TO BOUNCE BACK

Being resilient is about how we deal with difficult situations and bounce back from tough times. Difficulties are part of life—everyone has ups and downs. The good news is there are things you can do that can help you bounce back and be resilient!

Even if we feel happy, it doesn't mean we won't ever feel sad, angry, or lonely. Those feelings are normal if, for example, we've lost something or someone, or been hurt. Resilience is finding ways to manage those situations and feelings.

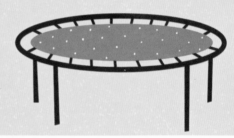

BENDING BUT NOT BREAKING

Think of a tree in the wind. It doesn't stay standing upright and stiff. If it did, it would soon break.

Instead, it bends under the pressure of the wind and it may even lose a few leaves. Then, when the wind stops, it becomes tall and stands straight again.

Being resilient is being like that tree. When we face difficult situations, it's not about staying stiff and pretending everything is okay. Instead, we "bend"—we feel sad or upset. There are lots of things we can do so we don't break and that can help us bounce back again.

TIPS: WAYS TO BE RESILIENT

Many of the activities in this book can help us be resilient. When you face difficulties, use the activities in this book and remember these tips:

Put things in perspective and think about the bigger picture. Are you making a mountain out of a molehill?

IF YOU FEEL ANGRY, UPSET, ANXIOUS, OR STRESSED...pause and take a few deep, slow breaths, in and out, focusing on your breath. This can help you feel calmer and help you choose what to do next in response.

GET ACTIVE and go for a walk or a run.

HAPPY FACT

Psychologists call resilience "ordinary magic" because we all have resilience and we can all develop more of it!

ASK FOR HELP when you need it.

PLEASE HELP!

FIND A SAFE ADULT or a good friend to talk to.

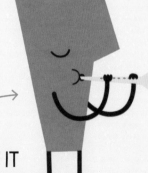

TAKE YOUR MIND OFF IT by doing something you enjoy or are good at, or by helping someone else.

32. BOUNCE-BACK BALLOONS

Here's a bouncy and fun way to give yourself a boost!

Blow up some balloons and grab a marker pen.

I ASKED FOR HELP

I WENT FOR A WALK

I DIDN'T PANIC

I TOLD MYSELF TO KEEP GOING

I TALKED TO MY FRIEND

I TRIED AGAIN

Think back to a tough time or a tricky situation that you coped with. On each balloon, write an action or a thought that helped you get through your tough time.

Ask an adult to think of a time when they "bounced back." Find out what it was that helped them. If any of these things could work for you, add them to your bounce-back balloons.

Tie some string or ribbon to your balloons and gather them into a bunch. With so many uplifting and positive actions in your hand, you've got lots of ideas to help you bounce back!

33. RESILIENCE SNAKES AND LADDERS

Do you know the board game snakes and ladders? If you roll the die and land at the bottom of a ladder, you can move up, but if you land on a snake, you must slide down to the bottom and move farther away from the finish line. Well that's what happens in life—everyone has ups and downs!

Play this game of "Resilience Snakes and Ladders" with your family and friends.

HOW TO PLAY

★ When a player lands on a square with a snake, they say something that they find difficult. They then move down the snake.

★ When a player lands on a square with a ladder, they say something that helps them "bounce back." They then move up the ladder.

HAPPY FACT

Not all stress is bad! We need a little stress to help us do our best.

34. RESILIENT COMIC STRIP

Everyone has difficulties. Even people who have success have had to deal with setbacks, rejections, and upsets. Using books, the internet, or by asking an adult, find out and think about someone who has overcome a difficulty, become stronger, and succeeded. This might be a famous athlete, someone from a film, or even someone you know.

Draw a comic strip to show how the person bounced back from a difficult time.

What ideas could be helpful for you?

35. MY RESILIENCE UMBRELLA

Knowing who we can go to for help is part of resilience. Like having an umbrella in the rain, other people can help us when we are struggling.

Who are the people (or the places) that you can turn to for help? These might be members of your family, teachers, other safe adults, or good friends. Draw a picture of an umbrella and write their names on it. Remember that different people can help with different things. Keep your resilience umbrella in a safe place for when you need it.

THERE ARE OTHER PLACES YOU CAN GET HELP TOO — SEE PAGE 62.

36. MAKE A RESILIENCE BOOKMARK

Make a handy bookmark that is also a useful reminder of activities to help you be resilient.

YOU WILL NEED:

- Cardstock
- Scissors
- Colored markers
- Stick-on stars

CREATE AND MAKE

HOW TO MAKE A RESILIENCE BOOKMARK

1 Cut out a long rectangle shape from the card.

2 On one side of the bookmark write the heading "BE RESILIENT" and list all the ways you can think of to be resilient (use the tips on page 41, or make up some of your own).

3 Decorate your bookmark however you wish.

50 WAYS to feel HAPPY

4 Use your bookmark as you work through this book and look at it to remind you of your ways to be resilient!

MY REMINDERS

ASK for help

TALK to someone

Get ACTIVE

Get BUSY

Take DEEP BREATHS

8 EMOTIONS

LOOK FOR WHAT'S GOOD

Being in a happy mood doesn't just feel good, it can do you good too!

When you're in a happy mood, you're more likely to be friendly and kind toward others. You're also likely to think creatively, see more options, and be open to information and ideas. Over time, these actions help you to build good relationships, learn more, be better at problem solving, be more resilient, and HAVE MORE FUN!

HAPPY FACT

Human brains are more likely to notice things that are wrong than things that are right. Our brains have evolved this way to help keep us safe. Training your brain to spot and remember the good things you see and experience can help you feel more happiness each day!

QUICK START: EXPERIMENT WITH SMILES

★ Smile at someone and see if they smile back.

★ Smile at yourself in a mirror for one minute. Does it change what you are feeling?

★ Set a friend a smile challenge! Look into each other's eyes. Your task is to smile at them a lot and their task is not to smile. See how long they can last!

★ What makes you smile?

TIP
Focusing on good things doesn't mean we should ignore unpleasant emotions such as fear, worry, sadness, or anger. All emotions give us signals that help us make sense of what we are experiencing.

HAPPY FACT

Scientists have found out that smiling can actually help us feel happier!

37. PUT ON A PLAY WITH EMOTIONS

Make up a story with a friend and try to fit in as many emotions as you can!

Put on a play and act out your story. Use costumes, props, and facial expressions to show the emotions your characters feel. Invite your friends and family over to watch it!

Fear

Anger

Guilt

Sadness

Confusion

Love

Joy

Gratitude

Surprise

Pride

Hope

THINK ABOUT IT

Think about each of the emotions below—have you ever felt each of them? When might each of these emotions be positive?

CAN YOU THINK OF ANY OTHER EMOTIONS?

38. CREATE A POSITIVITY PACK

★ Gather lots of things that help you feel pleasant or positive emotions. You could collect pictures, photos, drawings, souvenirs, songs, poems, stories, video clips, etc.

★ Find a place to keep these things together—for example a box, scrapbook, or on your computer. You could decorate your box or scrapbook to make it special.

★ If you're feeling sad or need a boost of positivity, look back at your pack.

★ Don't forget to add any new things you find!

HAPPY FACT

It's hard not to smile when someone smiles at you. This is because a smile is a signal that someone is friendly and wants to connect.

POSITIVITY

CREATE AND MAKE

GLASS HALF FULL OR HALF EMPTY?

In some situations, there are different ways we can look at things. For example, a glass filled halfway up with milk could be seen as half full or half empty.

While both are true, it can be helpful for happiness to look on the bright side and see what's good.

OH NO, SOMEONE'S ALREADY DRUNK HALF MY MILK!

LUCKY ME—HALF A GLASS OF MILK! JUST ENOUGH!

39. BE A HAPPINESS COLLECTOR!

Try this for a fun way to train your brain!

HOW TO DO IT:

★ Put a notebook and pen by your bed.

★ Each night for a week, before you go to sleep, think of three things you have enjoyed, were grateful for, or were pleased about during the day. Even the tiniest things count!

★ Write them in your notebook.

★ At the end of the week, look back over your list and remember all of the good things you've seen or felt.

HAPPY FACT

People who did this activity each night for one week had a happiness boost that lasted up to six months!

Why not ask your family or friends what their three good things are each day?

40. HAVE AN ATTITUDE OF GRATITUDE

Being thankful is a happiness superpower. Gratitude helps us appreciate what we have and what's around us and helps us to build connections with others.

Gratitude has two parts—**noticing** something good and **being thankful** for it and where it came from. There are lots of different ways to be grateful!

WRITE A LETTER OF GRATITUDE

Think of someone you are really grateful you have in your life. Write a letter to them saying why you appreciate them and what they have done for you. Be sure to include how it has helped and made a difference for you. Post it or read it aloud to them!

41. MAKE A GRATITUDE TREE

CREATE AND MAKE

How many things can you think of that you are grateful for in your life? Challenge yourself to come up with one thing for each letter of the alphabet!

YOU WILL NEED:

- Handful of small tree branches
- String or ribbon
- Small vase or pot
- Paper
- Scissors
- Hole punch
- Pens/pencils

ASK AN ADULT

1 Gather your tree branches into a bundle and place them in your vase so that they stand up tall like a tree.

2 Cut out 26 paper leaves from your paper.

3 Using your hole punch, make a hole in the corner of each of your leaves.

4 Write a different letter of the alphabet onto each of your leaves.

5 For each letter, think of something you are thankful for and write it on the leaf. If you can't think of something for one letter, leave it blank to fill in later.

6 Thread some string or ribbon through the hole in each leaf and hang on your tree.

7 Put your gratitude tree somewhere that you can notice it each day.

8 Encourage others to create their own gratitude trees, or make one as a group.

9 ACCEPTANCE

Everyone is different. That means we are all special!

BE COMFORTABLE WITH WHO YOU ARE

Do you focus more on what you do wrong or what you do right? Do you compare yourself to others and dwell on what you don't like about yourself?

Learning to accept who you are and making the most of your strengths is an important happiness skill. It's about treating yourself like you would a good friend!

HAPPY FACT

Every single person has strengths and weaknesses and everyone makes mistakes sometimes. We're all human!

QUICK START: "ME AT MY BEST"

Look at the sentences below and think of as many different endings as you can.

★ I felt proud of myself when I...

★ I am good at many things, including...

★ I am special because...

42. MAKE A PERSONAL ID CARD

What makes you unique? Make a personal ID card for yourself to show the things that add up to you being you.

DON'T COMPARE YOUR INSIDES TO OTHER PEOPLE'S OUTSIDES!

PICTURE OF ME

APPEARANCE
* Height: 44 inches (110 cm)
* Gender: Male
* Hair color: Brown
* Eye color: Green

INTERESTS / HOBBIES
* Tree climbing
* Skateboarding
* Reading
* Playing with my friends

THREE THINGS I DO WELL
* Being a good friend
* Being ready on time for school
* Skateboarding

ONE THING I FIND TRICKY
* Keeping my shoes clean

MY FAVORITE THINGS
* Color: Yellow
* Food: Pineapple
* Book: 50 Ways to Feel Happy
* Place: The beach

HAPPY FACT

Comparing things we don't like about ourselves to other people who we see as "perfect" can be harmful to our happiness. It's important to remember that no one is perfect and everyone is different.

STRENGTHS IN THE SPOTLIGHT

Strengths are the positive qualities people have. They might be things that they are naturally good at or personal qualities that make a difference to others and the world around them.

Our strengths influence what we enjoy doing and what we find easier to learn. Spotting, using, and developing our own strengths is a helpful happiness skill.

What do you love and get energy from doing? What do you find easy to learn and do? Answering these questions will help you discover your own strengths.

There are lots of different strengths we can have, for example, being:

kind   creative   generous
flexible
hard-working   forgiving
curious
funny   helpful   caring
considerate
energetic   thoughtful   determined
reliable   respectful   patient
practical   playful

43. YOUR SUPER-SELF PORTRAIT

Think of all of your strengths and the good things about you. Pick one or two of these and imagine yourself as a superhero who uses your strengths to save the day! Draw a picture of your super self and label it with all the good things about you.

HAPPY FACT

In a scientific experiment, people were asked to identify their top strengths and find new ways to use one of them each day. They practiced this for one week.

At the end of the week they had a small boost in happiness and this grew over the next six months because they became better at understanding their strengths and finding different opportunities to use them.

44. PUT YOUR TOP STRENGTHS TO WORK!

Once you know what your strengths are, it's time to put them to work. One really good way of using your strengths to help boost your happiness is to find ways to use them when you have to do something you don't like doing!

Using your strengths can help you feel happier, more confident, have more energy, and be more resilient. It can help you achieve your goals, too!

Choose one of your top strengths and use it to complete a task that you don't like doing, such as cleaning your bedroom.

For example:

...if you're creative:
★ Find and try out new ways to arrange your stuff neatly;
★ Collect and decorate a set of cardboard boxes to store your things.

...if you're energetic:
★ Clean your room as fast as you can! Keep a note of your times, and try to beat your fastest time whenever you have to clean;
★ Put on some lively music and dance your way to a tidy room!

45. TURN YOUR INNER CRITIC TO AN INNER FRIEND

Do you ever think or tell yourself things like "I'm so stupid" or "I'll never be any good" when things go wrong?

Being critical of yourself can make you feel unhappy, so try telling your inner critic to be kinder. Remember everyone has strengths and weaknesses. Things won't go perfectly all the time and you can always learn from mistakes.

NO ONE IS PERFECT! Everyone makes mistakes.

TIPS: BE A GOOD FRIEND TO YOURSELF

It's natural to want to improve and it's easy to think that the best way to do this is to focus on what you are not good at. But this can damage your happiness! Instead of criticizing, try to be a good friend to yourself.

★ Celebrate what's good about yourself by writing each of your strengths onto a sticky note and post them around your bedroom.

★ Start the day with a smile to yourself in the mirror.

★ When you are having a tough time, give yourself a hug!

★ If you mess up, remind yourself that everyone makes mistakes.

★ Think about what you could do differently next time. Try using your top strengths to help you find ways to improve, learn, and move on.

46. WRITE A LETTER TO YOURSELF

Think about a time when you messed up and you felt bad about yourself.

Write a kind letter to yourself as if you were writing to a friend who had messed up. You could include supportive advice and tips and reminders of your strengths and positive qualities.

Pop it in an envelope and keep it somewhere safe.

In the future, if you feel like you've made a mistake, you can find and read your letter to yourself.

10 MEANING

BE PART OF SOMETHING BIGGER

WE ARE ALL PART OF A BIGGER WORLD.

Meaning matters for happiness, but what does meaning mean?

Meaning is about knowing how you connect and contribute to the world around you. It's also about understanding that YOU and what you do matters. Meaning also means thinking bigger than your own happiness: it's about how you can help to make the world a happier place too!

Sometimes doing things that are meaningful can be hard work but, once achieved, can lead to a sense of fulfillment and pride.

HAPPY FACT

People who have a sense of meaning in their lives tend to feel happier. They are likely to have more positive emotions, better well-being, higher resilience, and more confidence.

QUICK START: THE WORLD AROUND YOU

How are you connected to the world around you? Think about your family and friends, your home, clubs or groups you are part of, your school, your pets, and the natural world around you—even the stars and sky above!

47. CREATE YOUR OWN COAT OF ARMS

Meaning can come from knowing your personal "story"—where you have come from, what you stand for, and how the different parts of your life fit together.

Some families and individuals have their own coat of arms—a shield or shape with different symbols to represent important things in their lives. Why not make your own?

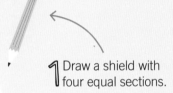

1 Draw a shield with four equal sections.

CREATE AND MAKE

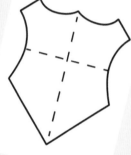

BE KIND AND FEEL HAPPY

2 In each of the sections, add a picture or symbol of things which have a strong meaning for you.

3 Include a personal motto (words or a phrase which represents your outlook on life) in a banner at the bottom of your shield.

DO YOU KNOW ANY DIFFERENCE MAKERS?

Think about a person you know who makes a difference to others or the world around them. For example, this might be someone who fundraises, volunteers for a charity, helps others learn, or looks after people or the environment.

How do you think this contributes to their happiness and the happiness of others?

Ask them about how their actions make a difference.

48. MAKE A DIFFERENCE

There are lots of ways you can make a difference to the world around you. For example...

* ★ Being patient or kind
* ★ Making people laugh
* ★ Picking up litter
* ★ Looking after animals or plants
* ★ Helping to cook dinner for your family
* ★ Creating a beautiful picture for someone to brighten their day
* ★ Recycling your trash
* ★ Volunteering or helping raise money for a charity

Pick one activity from this page, or think of your own way to make a difference around you. Ask an adult to help, if you need it.

49. MAKE A MEANING COLLAGE

Collect pictures of the most important sources of meaning in your life and use them to create a meaning collage! For example, you might collect photos of your friends and family, pictures of where you live and the things you do, images of your favorite places, books, songs, and games, or anything that's important to you and your life.

HOW TO DO IT:

★ Each time you discover something that has meaning for you, take a photo, draw, or find a picture.

★ When you have lots of pictures, think about why you chose each one and its meaning for you. You could write notes to go with each picture, or explain your pictures to a friend.

★ When you're ready, put your pictures together into a collage.

★ Give your collage a title and write one sentence about what is most important and meaningful for you in your life as a whole.

★ Display your collage where you can see it regularly.

Invite your friends to do the activity and share their pictures with you too!

CREATE AND MAKE

HAPPY FACT

Scientists have found that people who have several different sources of meaning in their life are more resilient.

50. MAKE A MEANING CHAIN

CREATE AND MAKE

Create a paper chain to hang around your room that shows things in your life that mean a lot to you and the ways you make a difference for others or the world around you.

YOU WILL NEED:

- Sheets of colored paper
- Scissors
- Pens and pencils
- Glue or sticky tape

HOW TO DO IT:

1 Cut the paper into equal sized strips (about 6 horizontal sections on a letter-size page).

3 Glue the first strip of paper into a ring.

4 Link the next strip through the ring and glue it to form a second ring.

5 Keep repeating this until you have joined all of your strips and made a paper chain.

6 Hang the chain around your bedroom and add to it as you think of more examples.

Each evening, look at your paper chain and think about the ways in which the links are important in your life. Add to your chain whenever you think of other meaningful things!

2 On each strip, write something or someone that means something to you, or a positive thing that you do or have done to make a difference.

My friends

I am kind

I love my mom

I look after my cat

Spending time with my family

I recycle my trash

PULLING IT ALL TOGETHER

Hopefully exploring happiness has been fun and you've discovered lots of different activities that can help you to feel happy.

You might have worked your way through each chapter, dipped in and tried activities here and there, or maybe you wanted to read the whole book first and then decide which ones to pick. The order and amount of activities you've tried doesn't matter, but hopefully you can now take the ten keys to happier living with you and use them in your daily life. Luckily, there's an easy way of remembering them, because the first letter of each of the keys together spell **GREAT DREAM**!

★ GIVING—Do things for others
★ RELATING—Connect with people
★ EXERCISING—Take care of your body
★ AWARENESS—Live life mindfully
★ TRYING OUT—Keep learning new things

★ DIRECTION—Have goals to look forward to
★ RESILIENCE—Find ways to bounce back
★ EMOTIONS—Look for what's good
★ ACCEPTANCE—Be comfortable with who you are
★ MEANING—Be part of something bigger

You could turn your favorite activities from this book into daily or weekly "happiness habits" and you could even share them with your friends and family. You might also save some activities and try them again later when you need an extra boost of happiness.

★ Which activities will you make your daily or weekly "happiness habits?"
★ Which activities will you keep for when you need a happiness boost?
★ Which activities could you teach your friends and family?

The important thing to remember is that you can make a difference! Even small actions can lead to a happier you... and a happier world!

HAPPINESS IS A JOURNEY, NOT A DESTINATION AND THERE'S LOTS OF FUN TO BE HAD ALONG THE WAY!

WHAT TO DO IF YOU FEEL VERY UNHAPPY

We all feel unhappy from time to time, that's normal. As well as trying some of the activities in this book, it can often help to find someone to talk to. If you have felt unhappy for some time, it's very important to ask for help and support.

There are a number of ways to get help:

★ Talk to a safe adult of your choice —someone you know that you can trust and who is able to help you find ways of solving the problem or support you to take action to get any help that you may need. This could be your mom, dad, caregiver, another family member, friend, teacher, school principal, school counselor, doctor, or faith group leader, etc. Can you think of any other safe adults who you could talk to?

(Note: Sometimes you may need to talk to more than one person from your list to get support or help.)

★ Contact a free and confidential helpline. In some states there are free telephone or online helplines that can help. You will need to find out what helplines are available in your area, and what type of children's worries they deal with.

NOTE TO PARENTS, CAREGIVERS AND TEACHERS

Research shows that we can learn skills to be happier. Of course, many factors impact how happy we feel, but the choices we make about our actions, thinking patterns, and attitudes play an important role.

The activities in this book can help your child learn skills to help them be resilient, live a happy life, and contribute to the happiness of others. It can be explored by the child on their own, or you can explore it together. You may even want to try some happiness actions for yourself.

If you want to find out more about happiness and psychological health, here are some great places to start...

ACTION FOR HAPPINESS

Backed by experts, Action for Happiness is a leading not-for-profit organization whose mission is to inspire individuals, schools, communities, and workplaces to take evidence-based action to create a happier, more caring world.
www.actionforhappiness.org

BOOK FOR ADULTS

10 Keys to Happier Living—A Practical Evidence-Based Guide by Vanessa King is an easy-to-read guide to the science of happiness and the practical actions we can take to foster it for ourselves and others—at home, in the office, and in our communities.
ISBN: 9781472233424 (Headline)

TOOLKIT FOR SCHOOLS

The Keys to Happier Living Toolkit for Primary Schools
is an engaging, accessible and evidence-based program to promote the emotional well-being and resilience of children aged 7-11.
www.actionforhappiness.org/toolkit

INDEX